Gh[osts]

Henri[k Ibsen]

Adapted by Jo[...] [...]

Literal translation by Charlotte Barslund

methuen | drama

LONDON • NEW YORK • OXFORD • NEW DELHI • SYDNEY

METHUEN DRAMA
Bloomsbury Publishing Plc
50 Bedford Square, London, WC1B 3DP, UK
1385 Broadway, New York, NY 10018, USA
29 Earlsfort Terrace, Dublin 2, Ireland

BLOOMSBURY, METHUEN DRAMA and the Methuen
Drama logo are trademarks of Bloomsbury Publishing Plc

First published in Great Britain 2023

Cover design by Rebecca Heselton

Cover image © Chuttersnap/ Unsplash

Typography by Typeland

A catalogue record for this book is available from the British Library.

A catalog record for this book is available from the Library of Congress.

ISBN: PB: 978-1-3504-5735-5
ePDF: 978-1-3504-5736-2
eBook: 978-1-3504-5737-9

Series: Modern Plays

Typeset by Mark Heslington Ltd, Scarborough, North Yorkshire
Printed and bound in Great Britain

To find out more about our authors and books visit
www.bloomsbury.com and sign up for our newsletters.

Ghosts by Henrik Ibsen, adapted by Joe Hill-Gibbins, had its world premiere at the Sam Wanamaker Playhouse, Shakespeare's Globe, on 10 November 2023 with the following cast and creative team:

Jakob Engstrand	Greg Hicks
Father Manders	Paul Hilton
Helene Alving	Hattie Morahan
Regine Engstrand	Sarah Slimani
Osvald Alving	Stuart Thompson

Adapter	Joe Hill-Gibbins
Artistic Director	Michelle Terry
Associate Director	Lucy Wray
Director	Joe Hill-Gibbins
Costume and Set Designer	Rosanna Vize
Costume Supervisor	Megan Rarity
Globe Associate, Movement	Glynn MacDonald
Head of Voice	Tess Dignan
Intimacy Director	Haruka Kuroda
Literal Translation	Charlotte Barslund
Script Editor	Lucy Wray

Special thanks to Lucy Wray.

Ghosts

a domestic drama in three acts

Characters

Regine Engstrand
Jakob Engstrand
Father Manders
Helene Alving
Osvald Alving

The action runs continuously, with no jumps in time.

I

Regine *strikes a match. She is lighting candles.* **Engstrand** *appears.*

Regine   No, sorry. You can't come in.

Engstrand *advances. He has a limp.*

Regine   I said: you can't come in. You're soaking wet.

Engstrand   God has opened up the heavens.

Regine   More like the devil's opened hell. What do you want?

Engstrand   I just need a minute. I've come to see you.

Regine   Shh – shh. Stop banging around with that leg. Mr Alving's asleep upstairs.

Engstrand   In bed? It's midday?

Regine (*continuing lighting the candles*)   That's none of your business.

Engstrand   The drink got a hold of me last night. Possessed me like a devil.

Regine (*in a French accent*)   *Quelle surprise.*

Engstrand   The flesh is weak.

Regine   The flesh is still drunk.

Engstrand   And yet, I was up at five thirty this morning for work.

Regine   And I was up at six. You win. Is that all you came to tell me?

Engstrand   I just need one minute with you.

Regine   I don't have time to *rendez vous*.

Engstrand   To what?

Regine   I don't want people seeing you here.

Engstrand   I have to talk to you. Today I finish on the children's home. Tonight I'm getting the ferry. I'll be gone.

Regine   *Bon voyage*.

Engstrand   I have to leave before the ceremony tomorrow. They'll be toasting it, see – with champagne. I can't have anything to do with that. The temptation would be too strong.

Regine *makes a dismissive noise.*

Engstrand   'Cause they'll be coming up from the town for it. Proper people . . . Father Manders.

Regine   He's coming here today.

Engstrand   Exactly. And I can't be getting drunk in front of him.

Regine   Why?

Engstrand   He's a man of God.

Regine   No, what do you want from him? What are you scheming?

Engstrand   Scheming? About the Father? That man's given me so much already: I couldn't ask for anything more.

Regine   Your minute's up. What do you want?

Engstrand   I'm going back to town today. And I want you to come with me.

Pause.

I want you to come with me.

Come live with me.

Regine   I live here. Mrs Alving's brought me up like family.

Engstrand   I'm your family.

Regine   Are you? That's not what you've said.

Engstrand   What?

Regine   'Not mine. Nothing to do with me.' That's what you said before.

Engstrand   When?

Regine   When you're drunk.

Engstrand   Well, then I'm drunk. The drink made me do it. The drink and your mother. Yes. I said it to get back at her. Pushing me, needling me, she was. Saying she's too good for me – just like you now. Up here in the big house for three years she was, and I never heard the last of it. 'Get your hands off me, don't touch me . . . I belong in Captain Alving's house.' Up here with Captain Alving not down there with shameful old me.

Regine   Well, she's dead now. Happy?

Engstrand   That's my fault, is it?

Regine   She died too young. Probably just to get away from you.

Pause.

Engstrand   You look just like her, you know.

Pause.

Regine   Why do you want me in town?

Engstrand   Why? Because you're my girl. Because you're all I have in the world.

Regine   And? . . . *And*?

Engstrand   I've had an idea.

Regine   Not again.

Engstrand   A new one.

Regine   A new disaster.

Engstrand   Not a disaster. Not this time . . . I've been saving
– money. Eight hundred Kroner.

Regine   I don't believe you.

Engstrand   I've been working non-stop. I built half that
children's home. And what is there to spend it on up here?

Regine   Go on.

Engstrand   I'm going to start a business. In town. It's a
kind of home for sailors.

Regine   Down the port?

Engstrand   A nice place. A classy place. Not some dump for
crew – for captains, officers. Proper people. A place to drink,
to stay, to – socialise.

Regine   And I would be . . .?

Engstrand   The face of the operation. A female face.
Greeting them after weeks at sea. You work fifteen-hour
days up here – you'd work four hours a night down there.
Easy life. You'd be free.

Regine   I'm not going back to town. And I'm not staying
here either. Trust me.

Engstrand   You've got to be smart, Regine. You live on the
estate, Mrs Alving put you through school, but now what?
They're like your family, but they're not your family. I heard
they're going to put you to work in the children's home. A
thousand bastard brats puking and crying. Is that what you
want? Is that your life?

Regine   Eight hundred Kroner?

Engstrand   For a new start. For us.

Regine   I need clothes. A new dress.

Engstrand   You can have any dress you want – if you come.

Regine   You think I can't do it on my own?

Engstrand   I think a father to guide you's better. In our new home. Our house for sailors.

Regine   I don't want to live with you. I don't want anything to do with you. Now – Ow!

Regine, *distracted by* **Engstrand**'s *proposition, has let a match burn down to her fingers. She is hurt.*

Regine   Ow!

Engstrand   My girl.

Regine   Get out. Leave!

Engstrand   Shh – shh – shh.

He moves to comfort her. He is touching her.

Hey. It won't be forever. I promise. I promise. If you play it smart. You're a beautiful girl now. A beautiful woman.

Regine   Am I?

Engstrand   Yes. And it won't be long before an officer – a captain even.

Regine   I don't want to marry a sailor. They've got no *savoir vivre*.

Engstrand   No one's talking about marrying them. You understand me? That Englishman – that captain, with the yacht – he ended up paying three hundred Kroner – three hundred for one night – and she was no better looking than you.

Regine   Get out. *Je te déteste!*

She pushes him. **Engstrand** *grips his leg.*

Engstrand   Ow! Don't hurt me. You wouldn't hurt me. I'm an old man.

Regine   You say one word about my mother ever again and I'll hit you so hard that shit leg'll be your best feature.

Engstrand   'Shh! Shh! Mr Alving's asleep – Shh! – Mr Alving's asleep' . . . Embarrassing. Can smell it on you a mile off.

Regine   Get out. Not that way, that way. I don't want the Father to see you here, you . . . Stain.

Engstrand (*leaving*)   Ask the Father about my proposition. I'm serious – and what will he say? 'Honour thy father and mother.' (*Returning.*) Because I am your father. No matter what. He wrote it in the parish register himself.

Father Manders *has appeared.* **Engstrand**'s *gone.*

Scene Two

Manders   Good morning, Miss Engstrand.

Regine   Good morning, Father. The ferry's been?

Manders   Been and gone. It was a rough crossing. It's lashing down.

Regine   God has opened up the heavens.

Manders   I'm sorry?

Regine   I mean . . . That's what we say up here.

Manders   Is Mrs Alving here? She's expecting me.

Regine   She's making coffee. Herself. For sir.

Manders   Sir? For Osvald? He's here?

Regine   Came back the day before yesterday. For the opening of the children's home.

Manders   And how is he? Is he well?

Regine   He's tired. He took the train all the way from Paris. And soaked on the boat of course. He's still in bed now.

Manders *has started to take off his boots.*

Regine   Can I help you with that, Father?

Manders   Oh – thank you.

She begins to unlace his boots. Short pause.

Manders   When did I last see you, Regine? You look – different.

Regine   What do you mean, Father?

Manders   I mean . . . You've matured.

Regine   Have I? I suppose I have. Do you think so, Father? Mrs Alving says I'm not a girl anymore.

Manders   She's right.

Short pause.

Regine   Shall I tell Mrs Alving you're here?

Manders   There's no rush . . . Tell me: how is your father?

Regine   He's his usual self.

Manders   But how often do you see him?

Regine   I'm up here at the house, so . . .

Manders *takes hold of* **Regine**.

Manders   He needs you, Regine. You know that. He needs someone to keep him on the right path. He came to see me in town. He confessed as much himself.

Regine   He's not said that to me.

Manders   You're the only family he has, Regine. You and he: you're bound together.

Regine   Mrs Alving needs me in the house. And from tomorrow in the children's home.

Manders   She'll understand. Come back to him.

Regine   It wouldn't look right: a young girl living with an old man.

Manders   But he's your father.

Regine *slowly takes off his second boot.*

Regine   If it was a nice place. With a proper person. A gentleman. That'd be different. Someone who would look after me, and in return, someone I could devote myself to. Look up to. Almost like their daughter . . . For someone like that I'd come back to town. If I'm honest it does get pretty lonely up here. But you'd know all about that, Father. You know what it is to be alone in this world. And I'd work very hard for someone like that, Father. I'm very – enthusiastic. For life . . . So you'll promise you'll tell me?

Manders   What?

Regine   If you think of a man like that. For me.

Manders   I'm sorry, Regine. But I don't know anyone like that.

Regine   Well . . . If anyone springs to mind.

Manders   I think you'd better tell Mrs Alving I'm here.

Helene *has appeared.* **Regine***'s gone.*

Scene Three

Helene   Welcome, Father.

Manders   Helene. Here I am – as promised. At your service.

Helene   Right on time. As always.

Manders   It wasn't easy to get away. I'm very busy in town. Meetings, boards . . . committees . . . sub-committees.

Helene   Yet you still manage to find time for me. I'm very grateful. Shall we get all the business done before lunch? . . . Where are your bags?

Manders   They're down at the harbour. I'll sleep there tonight.

Helene   So I still can't persuade you to stay the night?

Manders   No. Thank you. I'll stay there as usual. And it's so convenient for the boat back tomorrow.

Helene   Have it your way. You don't think that two people, at our age, are perfectly capable of controlling ourselves?

Manders   You're joking. And it's very funny. You're in a good mood.

He has picked up a book.

Because of the ceremony tomorrow? Or because Osvald's home?

He stares at the spine of the book.

Helene   The sunshine of my life's come back. He hasn't been home for two years – and now he's promised to stay for Christmas.

Manders   He must really want his mother. Why else would he come home from Rome, Paris. Such exotic places.

Helene   He's devoted to me. My sweet boy.

Manders   I'm glad to hear it. It would be sad if separation from you, and the life of the artist, had disfigured his natural instincts.

Helene   There's nothing wrong with his instincts, Father. There's nothing wrong with him at all. I want you to see him. I want to see if you recognise him. He'll be down soon.

Manders   Then in the meantime. Maybe you and I should get down to business.

Helene   Of course.

Manders   But before we do. (*Holding up the book.*) Whose is this? . . . Is this Osvald's?

Helene   It's mine.

Manders   It's not . . . And you're reading this?

Helene   That's what I tend to do with books.

Manders   Why are you reading this?

Helene   Because . . . Because I like it.

Manders   What do you like about it? Tell me. I'm interested (*He hands her the book.*) Does it make you a happier person? Does it make you a better person? Hm? . . . What's it about?

Helene   You know what it's about.

Manders   I don't.

Helene   You do. Of course you do.

Manders   I want you to tell me. What's it about?

Helene   . . . It's about . . .

Manders   Yes?

Helene   If you're so intrigued you can borrow it. (*Trying to hand it back to him.*) Here.

Manders   I don't want it.

Helene   Here. What? . . . It's just paper. It won't bite.

Manders   I said I don't want it.

Helene   I recommend Chapter 15.

He takes the book and throws it away from her.

Manders   You haven't answered my question: do you feel happier when you read this? Truthfully.

Helene   I . . . I feel calm.

Manders   Calm?

Helene   Because . . . It says things that I already think, already feel. There's nothing new in this book. Just what people already know, inside, if they're honest. But then people aren't honest.

She picks up the book.

Manders   In Rome and Paris perhaps, but not here. Not us. This is just fashion. We live an older truth.

Helene   Why are you so threatened by it?

Manders   I'm not threatened by it. I don't even have time to read it.

Helene   So then you don't know what you're talking about.

Manders   I've read about it. I know what it is.

Helene   If you read it you could have your own opinion.

Manders   I trust the word of others. I trust the word of those around me. That's how society works. I trust my community and the values that we share together. We protect each other. We watch over each other. Why don't you see that?

Helene *has no response this time.*

Manders (*taking the book*)   Look, I'm not saying that a book like this can't be . . . seductive. And I know that you're only trying to understand what's going in the world. The world you sent your son out into for so long. But . . .

Helene   But what?

Manders (*handing her the book back*)   I just wouldn't shout about it, if I were you. I don't want you to be the subject of gossip

Helene   Of course you're right.

Manders   Think about your responsibility to the children's home.

Helene   No, you're right. Thank you.

Manders   Good. So to business. I have all the paperwork with me. Everything's ready. I just need you to sign. It wasn't easy. Licensing, governance, finances: I had to push to get everything through. The authorities are painfully stringent when it comes to signing things off. But I did it. First there's the registered deeds to the property. Everything's listed: dormitories, classrooms, staff quarters, the chapel. Then secondly, there is the appropriation of the legacy, and the statutes of the foundation. 'The articles of association for the Captain Alving Children's Home.'

Helene   So . . . this is it.

Manders   Next are details of the savings account and interest-bearing capital we've put aside to cover the running costs.

Helene   Yes. Are you happy to oversee all of that?

Manders   Of course, but it's very important you understand it. I recommend we let the money sit in the savings bank for now, even though the rate of interest is not ideal: four per cent at six months' notice. Of course at a later date we can look to borrow against the property, but only if we can find a good mortgage – which of course would have to be a *first* mortgage – and one of undisputed security. But are you happy with that?

Helene   I'm sure you know best, Father.

Manders   There's only one more thing – I've been meaning to ask you for a while . . . How do you propose to deal with the insurance situation?

Helene   The . . .?

Manders   The question of insurance . . . Do you want the children's home insured? Or not?

Helene   I . . . Well, I insure everything here. The house, the personal property.

Manders   Obviously. Your own property. I do the same. But I don't need to tell you that the children's home is very different. Because the children's home is dedicated to a higher purpose. God's purpose . . . Now, speaking personally, I wouldn't find it in any way problematic to safeguard ourselves against all eventualities.

Helene   I agree.

Manders   But we're not the only people involved here.

Helene   We're not?

Manders   Of course not. Setting up an institution like this – for the most vulnerable children: the orphaned, the abandoned – that brings with it . . . scrutiny. And that in turn brings the opinions of others. Important people, powerful people.

And the opinions of all those that vote for them.

Helene   The children's home is a memorial, in my late husband's name. It is funded entirely by his wealth.

Manders   But that won't protect us against people who might take offence?

Helene   Offence?

Manders   And in the town those people are everywhere. Just think of supporters of my enemies on the council. You do understand that spending all this money on insurance opens us up to an accusation. The accusation that you and I lack *faith*? . . . After all, we're doing God's work up here, so will not God protect us?

Beat.

Of course our conscience is clear, but that won't stop the misinterpretation of others. I've acted as your advisor and business manager here, and that's something people can use against me. Of course it's of huge benefit to the town – and significantly reduces their welfare spending – but that doesn't mean I'm not exposed. Exposed to opponents who'll say that I don't believe God will protect those children. I don't want to risk any kind of scandal that might affect –

Helene (*overlapping*)   Scandal?

Manders   In public, or behind closed doors. Attacks and insinuations undermining my work. It could be very damaging. You understand that don't you, Helene?

Helene   Of course.

Manders   So the question is: do you want the children's home insured – or not?

Helene   I . . . No.

Manders   Because it has to be your decision.

Helene   I'm sure. My mind's made up.

Manders   But if an accident were to happen – God forbid – would you have the funds to repair the damage?

Helene   No. No I wouldn't.

Manders   You do realise how big a responsibility you're taking on?

Helene   Do you think we have any other choice?

Manders   No. No, I don't believe we do. But I do have faith that God will grant us special protection. So it's settled.

Helene   Yes.

Manders   No insurance.

Helene   It's strange that you should bring this up today.

Manders   Why?

Helene   Because there was a fire there yesterday.

Manders   What?

Helene   A small one. A false alarm. A pile of sawdust caught fire. In the carpenter's shop.

Manders   Where Engstrand works?

Helene   He smokes constantly. Twenty cigarettes a day, that's twenty matches.

Manders That man's plagued by temptation on all sides. But I know he tries. I know he prays.

Helene How do you know?

Manders He told me himself. He works hard too.

Helene When he's not drunk.

Manders His leg makes him drink – he's in such pain. He came to see me in town. He thanked me for getting him the job here, so he could be with Regine.

Helene He hardly sees her.

Manders He needs her. He's nothing but honest about his weakness. And not afraid to ask for help. I think he needs his daughter, Helene. At home.

Helene No.

Manders Don't stand in the way.

Helene I will. I need Regine up here – in the children's home.

Manders But he's her father.

Helene Then he should act like it.

Manders You can't sever that bond – between parent and child.

Helene Regine stays here. She belongs here.

Osvald *has appeared. He is smoking.*

Scene Four

Osvald Sorry. I didn't know you were in here.

Manders *stares at* **Osvald**.

Helene Well? What do you think of him, Father?

Manders Is that really you?

Osvald It really is. Hello, Father.

They embrace.

Osvald   The return of the prodigal son.

Manders   No.

Osvald   The return of the son then.

Manders   Welcome home, Osvald.

Helene   Osvald was reminding me how you tried to stop him becoming a painter.

Manders   That's not true. I have no problem with artists. I just advised you to take care. That world can be . . . And those people. I just worry they don't have your best interests at heart.

Osvald   But you do.

Helene   Don't worry about his heart, Father. Or any part of him. He's just as perfect as the day he left.

Osvald   All right, mother.

He puts out his cigarette.

Manders   You're making quite a name for yourself. The toast of the art world. Though I haven't seen anything in the papers for a while.

Osvald   I haven't been painting much.

Helene   Artists need to rest – recharge. Find inspiration.

Manders   I'm sure that's right. Readying yourself for your next masterpiece, eh?

Osvald (*to* **Helene**)   When are we going to eat?

Helene   Half an hour. He's still got his appetite.

Manders   And a taste for nicotine.

Osvald   I found Daddy's silver lighter in the attic. Here.

He shows it. Sparks a flame.

And then I . . .

He lights a cigarette.

Manders   That's it.

Helene   What?

Manders   When he's smoking I see his father. Standing right there.

Osvald   Really?

Helene   No. He takes after me.

Manders   He looks identical.

Helene (*taking the cigarette out of* **Osvald**'s *mouth and extinguishing it*)   Please no more smoking. Inside, anyway.

Osvald (*looking at the lighter*)   I just wanted to try it. I haven't smoked since I was a child.

Helene   What?

Osvald   Yes. I did. I don't know how old I was. I was young. Six, seven. It was in here. I saw Dad smoking. He seemed so . . . happy.

Helene   You can't remember that far back

Osvald   Yes. He sat me on his lap. 'Here,' he said . . . 'Suck' . . . 'Good boy'. And I smoked. One – two puffs. Three. I felt so sick – I had sweat pouring down my face. And he was – laughing.

Helene   This is just a dream.

Osvald   You were there. You came in – carried me to my bedroom. I threw up. You were crying. Did he often do things like that?

Manders   He loved his silly jokes. When he was young. He grew out of all that. Think of everything he achieved for the town – the community.

Osvald   He did so much, didn't he? Even though he wasn't here for long.

Manders   You've inherited a great name, Osvald Alving. That should inspire you.

Osvald   It should do, yes.

Manders   Tomorrow, you'll feel so proud.

Helene   And after that I get to keep him until Christmas.

Manders   You're staying?

Osvald   I haven't bought a ticket back. It's good to be home.

Helene (*embracing* **Osvald**)   Isn't it?

Manders   You were so young when you left.

Osvald   I was. Sometimes I think too young.

Helene   No. It's good to get out in the world. Especially an only child. If you'd stayed home we'd have spoilt you.

Manders   With respect, Helene, I don't know that's true. The proper place for a child is at home with his parents.

Osvald   I agree with you, Father.

Manders   Just look at your own son. What's been the effect on him? He's 23 years old and he's never known a proper home.

Osvald   What do you mean?

Manders   That you left here so young, you were barely –

Osvald   No, the part about a proper home.

Manders   I mean you've been with young people. In artistic circles.

Osvald   Yes?

Manders   Not people, I imagine, prioritising marriage – building a home.

Osvald   They have homes. Where d'you think they live? Under a table in an opium den?

Manders   Very funny. I'm talking about family homes.

Osvald   How do you define family?

Manders   That's easy: a mother, a father and their children.

Osvald   Lots of my friends have children.

Manders   In a marital home?

Osvald   In all sorts of homes. With a mother and father, or just a mother, a father and a father, a mother and mother, or a community –

Manders (*overlapping*)   My point is that's different.

Osvald   Your point is that's worse. But I've seen all kinds of families full of love and warmth and care –

Manders   It's important for a child to grow up with a father and a mother. Surely *you* can't deny that.

Osvald   I think it's love that makes a home, Father. And love doesn't always follow your rules.

Helene   I agree with Osvald.

Manders   I know this is unpalatable to you but broken homes make broken people.

Osvald   Why don't you come visit us, Father. Join us on a Sunday.

Manders   Sunday is the Lord's Day.

Osvald   Sundays are when we're all together. Friends, their children. Cooking, talking, playing.

Manders   Drinking alcohol. Taking drugs. What a utopian vision. Parenting requires discipline, sacrifice. This 'freedom' you describe is just self-gratification. Tell me: your friends with children, are they the same artists who paint under-age prostitutes?

Osvald   You seem to know a lot about what goes on in
Paris, Father? Did you hear that from your friends? Model
husbands and fathers, returning from their travels abroad
with warnings of vice and debauchery.

Manders   I've heard stories, yes.

Helene   So have I.

Manders   So I have good reason to be worried about
your son.

Osvald   You know, sometimes when those men come to
Paris on business they even do the honour of joining us poor
artists for a drink. And they drink, and they drink, and they
tell us all about places and things we never even dreamed of.
So when they tell you all about 'the vice of Paris', you should
believe them, Father. Trust me, they're experts.

Helene   Osvald.

Osvald   And yet they dare, they *dare,* to come back here
and call the way we live immoral. To take our lives, that are
beautiful, loving and free, and smear them with their filth.

Helene (*overlapping*)   Osvald. It's alright, my darling. Don't
make yourself sick.

Osvald   You're right, mother. You're right . . . I get so tired.
I need to stop. I'll go for a walk – get some air. I'm sorry,
Father. This . . . Thing. It takes me over . . . I'm sorry.

He goes.

Scene Five

Helene   My poor boy.

Manders   His soul is lost.

Beat.

He called himself the prodigal son. He understands that.

Beat.

And what about you? You've nothing to say about that?

Helene Every word he said is true.

Manders True?

Helene Since I've been alone I've started to think like him, Father. But I've been too scared to say it. Now my son will speak for me.

Manders I feel sorry for you. But I can't let that stop me. I'm not your business advisor standing before you now. I'm not the old friend of your husband. I am your priest. The priest that stood before you in the most desperate moment of your life.

Helene And what does my priest want to say?

Manders I want you to remember what you did. It's time. Tomorrow's ten years to the day your husband died. Tomorrow we dedicate the children's home to his memory. Tomorrow I'll speak of him in public, but tonight I speak only to you. One year into your marriage when you came to me. You were desperate, on the verge of collapse. You'd abandoned your home, abandoned your husband. He pleaded with you to come home but you would not.

Helene Then you must remember too how unhappy I was . . .

Manders Unhappy? You made a sacred oath to love and honour him.

Helene You know the kind of man I married.

Manders The man you *married*. Committed to, before God – before me. What did those words mean to you, Helene?

Helene You know the way he treated me. Others too.

Manders He was young. So were you. He made mistakes. So did you. It was your place to help him – not to judge him. To carry him through. But instead you were selfish. Selfish and reckless. You pushed aside the man you were bound to help. And you put your reputation at risk – the reputation of others.

Helene   You mean you.

Manders   You never should have come to me.

Helene   I had nowhere to go. You were my friend. You were my priest.

Manders   I was. And I thank the Lord that I had the strength to do what was right. To talk you out of your wild ideas. To lead you back to your lawful husband.

Helene   That's true: you sent me back to him.

Manders   I was directed by a higher power. To bend you to obedience, to surrender, to service. And look at all the good that followed. He grew up – turned his back on that behaviour. You had years of happy marriage. Years of partnership – everything you did for the town, together. And you had a son. But that brought you to your second greatest sin.

Helene   What do you mean?

Manders   First you refused to be a wife, and then you refused to be a mother. The only thing you care about is doing whatever you want. You want to be free. No commitments. No sacrifice. Any obligation that gets in your way you trample over. Anyone that inconveniences you gets shoved aside. Being a wife didn't suit you: you walked out of your marriage. Being a mother was too great an imposition: you sent your child to be brought up by strangers.

Helene   Yes, that's true. That's what I did.

Manders   And now you're a stranger to him.

Helene   No. I'm not.

Manders   Yes you are. How could you not be. Don't lie to yourself. Face it. You sinned against your husband, but now you've built a memorial to make it right. You've sinned against your son but there's still time to save him. Repent your sins and turn him back from immorality – from death.

You are responsible. You are his mother. The guilt resides with you.

Silence.

Helene   You've had your say, Father. Now I want to talk.

Manders   Excuses will not help your son.

Helene   I want to speak.

Short pause.

The first year of our marriage you used to visit us every day. Do you remember, Father? Every single day. But after you sent me back to my husband, you never set foot in our house again.

Manders   You left the town, came up here.

Helene   Yes and you never came to visit. Not once. Not when my husband was alive. The first time you came here was to discuss the children's home.

Manders   Helene, you know who I am, you know my position –

Helene (*overlapping*)   Yes and God forbid that's tarnished by a reckless woman – by a runaway wife.

Manders   Enough hysterics.

Helene   Yes. Let's just deal in facts. Facts about fourteen years of 'happy marriage' you sent me back to. Fourteen years of happy marriage that you weren't here for one single day of.

Manders   Make your point.

Helene   How do you know we were happy?

Manders   Your work together flourished; you had a son.

Helene   I swore one day I'd tell you the truth – only you – and now that day is here.

Manders   Then say it.

Helene   My husband died a sinner. He sinned his whole life.

He never 'found his way back to the light', Father. No he drank, and drank, and lied, and cheated and cheated and cheated.

Manders   That's not possible. When he was young, perhaps but . . .

Helene   How do you think he died, Father?

Manders   . . . I don't understand.

Helene   No you don't – because our marriage was a lie, from start to finish.

Manders   I don't believe you – sorry. You couldn't keep this secret. People would have known.

Helene   People didn't know because I made sure they didn't know. It got a little better after Osvald was born. But it didn't last. Then I had to fight twice as hard to make sure no one knew what kind of man my baby's father really was. Everyone loved him of course – so generous, so charming – but I couldn't let anyone see the real him. I tried to keep him here as much as possible – stop him drinking in town. I became his accomplice.

Shut away with him up here, drinking with him night after night. It felt endless –- listening to whatever obscenity poured out of his mouth. Bragging about his conquests. Every night I had to fight, to get him off me and into bed.

Manders   But how could you bear this?

Helene   I had to. For my little boy. I found a way. Even when – when he . . .

Manders   When he what?

Helene   I could block out the affairs outside the house. But when I kept him here, he brought them home.

Manders   Home?

Helene   I was in here when I heard it. I heard Johanna – Regine's mother – making dinner through there. I heard him come in. He was saying something to her. I could tell he was drunk. She was whispering . . . I can hear them now. It was devastating. Humiliating. I heard her whisper, 'No. Leave me alone. Please.'

Manders   I don't condone it of course, but he was playing with her – fooling around.

Helene   No. He'd had her. And soon there was evidence even you could not ignore.

Manders   But here, in this house?

Helene   Here. Here with my boy. It was then I made a vow: to make this stop. I took control. Of him, the house, of everyone. Because now I had a weapon against him: proof of the affair. He couldn't resist. It was then I sent Osvald away. He was almost seven. He would notice things, see things, ask questions. I couldn't bear it, Father. I knew he would be poisoned here – breathing in this tainted air. So now you know why I sent him away. And now you know why he never set foot here again while his father was alive. But no one knows how much that's cost me.

Manders   You've been truly tested, Helene.

Helene   I couldn't have got through it without my work. I worked, non-stop. All of Captain Alving's success: the acquisition of property, the charity foundations – do you honestly think he was capable of that? He was passed out on the sofa. I drove everything. On his brighter days I dressed him up and sent him into town, but I took him back home before he had the chance to collapse into his drink and self-pity.

Manders   And this is the man you've built a memorial to?

Helene   For years I've lived in fear of the truth coming out. The things they'd call me. The stain on Osvald's name. The children's home is a permanent monument to Alving's goodness. It will kill off all the rumours, it'll bury any doubts.

Manders   It must.

Helene   There's another reason too. I don't want Osvald to inherit a single penny from his father. Nothing. All the money I've invested in the children's home, year upon year, it adds up to – and I've calculated this precisely – the exact amount of money Alving had the day I married him. That was the price that I sold myself for. Every penny of it I've spent on the children's home. Everything Osvald inherits, he gets from me. Nothing of his father will remain.

Scene Six

Osvald *is here.*

Osvald   This rain is eternal.

Helene   You're back already.

Osvald   It's chucking it down.

Helene   My poor boy. Are you freezing?

Osvald   I'm hungry.

Regine *is there.*

Regine   Lunch is served.

Helene   Good. Yes. We're coming. We just need a moment.

Regine   Would Mr Alving like me to open the red or white?

Osvald (*approaching* **Regine**)   Both, Regine. Both.

Regine   *Très bien, monsieur.*

Osvald   I better help you get them open.

Manders   I don't know how I can speak tomorrow knowing this.

Helene   You'll manage. Toe the line. You're good at that.

Manders   People must never know.

Helene   Exactly. Let's get this done. After tomorrow his ghost will be gone from this house.

Osvald *kisses* **Regine**.

Helene   It'll be like he never existed. There'll only be mother and son.

Helene *stops in her tracks. She's seen* **Osvald** *and* **Regine** *kissing.* **Regine**, *unaware of* **Helene** *watching, pushes* **Osvald** *off her and whispers:*

Regine   Sir . . . No. Let me go. Please . . .

Osvald *continues to kiss her.*

Manders   What is it?

Helene   The dead have come back . . . Johanna. And Alving.

Manders *can now see the couple too.*

Manders   But . . .

Helene   They're ghosts. They're his son and his daughter.

Manders   You mean that . . . Regine is . . .? . . . but then Osvald and she are . . .?

Helene   Don't say a word. (*Speaking so* **Osvald** *and* **Regine** *hear.*) I hope you're hungry, Father.

Manders   I . . .

Helene   Let's get you some wine. Osvald? Are you joining us?

Osvald   No. Thank you. I'm going outside to smoke.

Osvald *and* **Regine** *resume kissing.*

Helene   Good. I mean – at least it's stopped raining. Regine? . . . Regine?

Regine *prises* **Osvald** *off her.*

Regine   Yes, madam.

Helene   You can leave us. Go upstairs and start folding the hymn sheets for tomorrow.

Regine   Yes, madam.

Regine *leaves.*

Scene Seven

Manders   I feel sick. I can't even think about food.

Helene   What are we going to do?

Manders   I have no experience of – anything like this.

Helene   I'm sure we're not too late. That they've not . . .

Manders   No. God forbid. It's unnatural.

Helene   It's nothing. It's an infatuation. It's nothing.

Manders   Why are you asking me? I don't know anything about – that.

Helene   She has to leave.

Manders   Tonight.

Helene   But where to? We can't just put her on the street.

Manders   She should go to her father, of course.

Helene   To who?

Manders   Her father: Engstrand –. No, this isn't possible. Engstrand is her father.

Helene   Johanna confessed it. He didn't deny it. She left that night.

Manders   She was pregnant?

Helene   I gave her money. A lot of money. I made her promise never to say a word. When she got to town she did the rest. She looked up an old acquaintance: Engstrand. Told him some story about getting pregnant by an officer or admiral, and getting paid off. She and Engstrand married straight away. Well, you married them yourself.

Manders   He came to me. He was distraught. Wracked by guilt. He begged me to marry them. He said they were engaged.

Helene   He wanted her. And he wanted the money.

Manders   He lied to my face. For money! How much did you give her?

Helene   Three hundred.

Manders   Marrying a fallen women for three hundred Kroner.

Helene   You married me to a fallen man.

Manders   That's completely different.

Helene   You're right. He got three hundred, I got the whole estate.

Manders   You were engaged, you were in love.

Helene   I was in love. I was in love with you.

Manders   If I'd known I wouldn't have come so often. I wouldn't have visited every day.

Helene   I didn't want to marry him. My mother did the sums, you know. Wrote it down, showed me what the marriage was worth. I felt I had no choice.

Manders   Your marriage was entered into freely. In the sight of God, in accordance with all laws.

Helene   I'm done with laws. God's or anyone else's.

Manders   That's enough.

Helene   I never should have kept his secrets. I should have told the world what my husband was. But I was afraid – of what everyone would say: 'She left him first. She betrayed *him*.'

Manders   And you don't think that's true?

Helene   If I wasn't such a coward I'd tell Osvald the truth. Just as I told you. This was your father, the great Captain Alving.

Manders   You're scaring me, Helene.

Helene   Oh, don't worry. I'll say nothing – nothing because I'm a coward. A coward.

Manders   It's not cowardice to protect your son. It's natural that a boy loves his father.

Helene   Is it natural Osvald loves a lie?

Manders   Listen to your conscience. Osvald idolises him. He longs for his family. You estranged him from his father once, don't do it again.

Helene   But I've lied to him his whole life.

Manders   There's a reason you created this illusion.

Helene   Letter after letter, year after year.

Manders   Your son needs his father.

Helene   I don't know . . . But I do know that he cannot be with Regine. It would destroy them both.

Manders   I forbid it.

Helene   But then if I knew he was serious. If he – liked her. If it would make him happy . . .

Manders   What?

Helene   Maybe if I weren't such a coward I'd say: marry her. Or don't marry her, but *be* with her. Do whatever you want, but be happy and no more lies.

Manders   Lord God have mercy on your soul. I would never sanction such a marriage. Never.

Helene   Do you honestly think that's never happened? Hand on heart, do you honestly think you've never met a couple that's related like them?

Manders   I don't know what you mean.

Helene   Even up here?

Manders   Listen, I don't think . . .

Helene   What?

Manders   I think . . . Look, in some families things might not always be as clear cut as they should be, but the fact that you, as a mother, would tell your son to –

Helene   I won't. I won't say that to him.

Manders   But why? Because you're a coward? Not because it's wrong, perverted – against nature, against God – but because you're afraid?

Helene   Yes. Because I feel so frightened. Every day. Too frightened to speak, to act . . . I see them everywhere, Father . . . Ghosts. Like Osvald and Regine in the next room. The dead come back to life. Sometimes I think we're all dead, Father. Dead but still alive. It's not just our parents coming back in us. We're full of dead laws and dead beliefs. Dead ideas about how to live. I reach for people, and dead words fall from their mouths. There're ghosts everywhere, Father. They're here right now. And we're all so pathetically frightened. We can't break free.

Manders   Put down those evil books, Helene. Let go of
your deceitful plans. Of your rebellion. Come back towards
the light.

Helene   I can see the light, Father. I see it thanks to you.
When I stood before you – when you pushed me away. When
you sent me back to a life that was all lies – that you knew was
lies . . . I had to understand why you did that. Why you felt
what I felt, but couldn't admit it. Why you held up as right
and true everything I knew, inside, was wrong. Duty,
convention, shame . . . It was you made a rebel out of me.

Manders   What I did was right, Helene. It was the greatest
battle of my life. The battle against myself. But I won.

Helene   No you lost. It was a crime against us both.

Manders   You were crying, you were – wild. You said to me
. . . 'I'm here . . . Take me . . . Have me . . .' When I led you
back – when I said to you, 'Go back to your lawful husband',
was that a crime?

Helene   Yes. I think it was.

Manders   I don't understand you.

Helene   I think you did. Once. That night.

Manders   Helene, listen to me . . . Listen. I have never . . .
never . . . even in my most secret thoughts, ever thought of
you as anything but another man's wife.

Helene   Is that true?

Manders   Yes.

Helene   How easily we forget who we were.

Manders   No. I'm the same as I always was.

Helene   . . . Yes. Yes. Yes . . . Either way, those people are
dead. Now you're just a man who talks about insurance, and
I'm just a woman seeing ghosts . . .

Manders   We can't allow Osvald and Regine to be together.

Helene She must marry someone else. We'll find her a good match.

Manders As soon as possible. She's ready. Of age. Not that I notice things like that.

Helene She matured young.

Manders She did, didn't she. I could see – when I prepared her for confirmation – that she was . . . Developed. But first, she must go home to her father. No, Engstrand is not her father. I cannot believe he lied to me!

Engstrand *is here.*

Scene Eight

Engstrand I do beg your pardon.

Manders You.

Helene Good evening, Mr Engstrand.

Engstrand None of the maids were here. I took the liberty of coming in.

Helene Is there something I can help you with?

Engstrand No. But thank you. It's the Father I have business with.

Manders You want to talk to me?

Engstrand I do.

Manders About what?

Engstrand Well . . . I wanted to tell you: we've all been paid down there now – thank you very much, madam. And as we all worked so hard on it together, maybe we should finish it all off with little service down there, led by your good self.

Manders At the children's home.

Engstrand   Yes. But if you don't think that's appropriate . . .

Manders   Of course I do. But –

Engstrand   I say a prayer there every evening myself.

Helene   Do you?

Manders (*simultaneously*)   Do you?

Engstrand   Most nights. To ask for help. But I'm just a common man, of course. I don't have the proper words, God forgive me. But then I thought: as the Father's here . . .

Manders   First you must answer a question, Engstrand.

Engstrand   A question?

Manders   Do you possess the correct state of mind for such a blessing? Is your conscience clear?

Engstrand   My conscience? Right. Conscience is a messy business, Father.

Manders   I am ready to hear your confession.

Engstrand   I'm not sure there's quite time for that.

Manders   I want the truth. About Regine.

Helene   Father.

Engstrand   Regine? Has something happened to her?

Manders   You are her father, are you not?

Engstrand   Right. The Father knows about me and Johanna. God rest her soul.

Manders   No more evasion. Johanna confessed everything to Mrs Alving.

Engstrand   She did, did she?

Manders   I've found you out, Engstrand.

Engstrand   Thing is, she promised me she didn't.

Manders   And all these years you've concealed the truth from me. From *me*, who placed all my faith in you, unconditionally.

Engstrand   Yes, Father. I'm afraid I have.

Manders   How could you do this to me, Engstrand? I've always supported you – done everything I could for you. Answer me.

Engstrand   I'd have been sunk so many times without Father Manders.

Manders   And this is my reward? I have set down a lie in the parish register because of you. Year upon year you deceived me – abused my trust. This is it for you and me, Engstrand. I want nothing more to do with you – and no, don't try and change my mind. I don't want another word from you: this is the end.

Pause.

Engstrand   May I just have permission to ask you one tiny question?

Beat.

Have you ever done anything that, in the eyes of another man, might be considered a sin?

Beat.

And Father, is it not man's holy duty to raise up those who've fallen?

Manders   Yes. Yes it is.

Engstrand   Thank you, Father. And is it not also the duty of a man to keep his word?

Manders   Yes. Yes it is a man's duty to keep his word.

Engstrand   Then imagine, Father – just imagine, if you can – that a fallen woman had come to you. What would you have done? . . . Is it right for us men to judge a weak woman

so harshly? When Johanna had been abused by that
Englishman – or was he American? Or Russian? Anyway, she
was all alone, Father. She was desperate. Thing is, the poor
girl had rejected my advances once or twice in the past,
because there she was a beautiful girl and here I am with this
dodgy leg. You remember how I got my injury don't you,
Father – I know you do. I'd ventured into a dance hall,
minding my own business – except handing out the odd
Christian pamphlet on temperance and moderation –

Manders   And a crew of drunken sailors threw you down
the stairs. I know, Engstrand – you've bragged of this before.

Engstrand   No, it hasn't made me proud, Father. Far from
it. But anyway what I wanted to tell you was this: when poor
Johanna came to me, confided in me, she was crying her
eyes out. And I must confess, that truthfully, in my heart . . .
I felt sorrow for her.

Manders   And then?

Engstrand   Then I took her hands and I said to her: 'That
American's off on the seven seas and he's left you here poor
girl, a fallen creature and sinner. But I will do my duty . . .' I
raised her up, Father – raised her up and wed her, so no
one'd ever know the shame she suffered.

Manders   But you did this for money, Engstrand. She had
money which you took from her.

Engstrand   Money? Me? Not a single coin.

Manders (*looking to* **Helene**)   But you said that –

Engstrand   Hold on. Yes, I remember now. Johanna did
have a few coins on her, now you mention it – but I wanted
nothing to do with that. I said: 'Mammon, the wages of sin.'
I said, 'Let's go find that American – throw it back in his
face'. But of course he was gone. Across the ocean, Father. So
Johanna and I agreed that every Kroner should be spent on
bringing up that child – and so it was. Every single Kroner.

Manders   Is that true, Engstrand?

Engstrand   As God is my witness. I strove every day to be a father to that child, for all my weakness. My girl, Regine. And we had a happy life, together: her, me and Johanna, God rest her soul.

A happy life . . . You know, I never thought I'd be here telling this to you, Father. For if Jakob Engstrand's done a good deed in this world, he's kept it to himself. Stayed humble. Truth is: we're all weak, Father. Conscience . . . it's a messy business.

Short pause.

Manders   Jakob Engstrand. Give me your hand. Your hand.

Engstrand   Oh Lord, no.

Manders *grasps* **Engstrand**'s *hand.*

Manders   I humbly ask for your forgiveness. With all my heart. I'm sorry I misjudged you. If there was only something I could do – something as a symbol of my sincere regret.

Engstrand   Would the Father do that?

Manders   With the greatest of pleasure.

Engstrand   Only there is something. An opportunity. I'm thinking of setting up a kind of sailors' home, in town.

Helene   A sailors' home?

Engstrand   A refuge. For the wandering sailor. Temptations are manifold for those boys, see, but there, in that house, I'll look after them. I'll be like a father to them.

Manders (*to* **Helene**)   Well? What do you say to that?

Engstrand   I don't have a great deal of funds for the project, God knows, but if somehow there was a helping hand . . .

Manders   Yes, we must discuss this in detail, Engstrand. It's a fantastic idea. You go ahead and light the candles in the children's home. We're all in the right frame of mind now for evening prayers.

Engstrand   We are, aren't we. (*Leaving.*) Well, goodbye, madam. Take good care of my Regine for me, won't you? (*Returning.*) Dear Johanna's child . . . It's like she's in my blood. (*Pointing at his heart.*) Here. It really is.

Engstrand's *gone.*

Manders   And you have nothing to say to that man, Helene? He gave a quite a different explanation to yours, didn't he?

Helene   He really did.

Manders   You see how very careful one must be not to judge another.

Such a joy to be proven wrong though, isn't it?

Pause.

Helene   You're like a child.

Manders   What? . . . Me?

Helene *throws her arms around* **Manders**, *gripping him tightly.*

Manders (*quietly, struggling with her*)   No. No.

Helene   Don't be scared of me.

Finally he pushes her off him. **Helene** *falls to the floor.*

Manders   You're so – impulsive. You have such an exaggerated way of expressing yourself . . . So. I'll take the documents back with me . . . Please look after Osvald when he's back.

Manders *is gone.*

Scene Nine

Osvald *is here. He's drinking.*

Osvald Hello, mother.

Helene You're here. I thought you'd gone out.

Osvald Just for a cigarette . . . It's freezing out there . . . You've been in here with Father Manders?

Helene He's gone now. To the children's home.

Osvald Hm.

Helene Don't you want to come in here with me?

Osvald I'm not allowed to smoke.

Helene Well . . . Maybe just one.

Osvald Alright: I'll join you. Where did the Father go?

Helene I told you. The children's home.

Osvald Oh yeah. That's right . . . You two not hungry?

Helene Did you eat?

Osvald I did. It was very cosy. Just me. Sitting at my mother's table, in my mother's house, eating my mother's food.

Helene My baby boy . . .

Osvald Besides, what else is there to do? I can't paint here.

Helene Why not?

Osvald It's too dark. Look out the window. Not a single ray of sunlight. I hate it when I can't work.

Helene Maybe you shouldn't have come back here.

Osvald Oh, but I had to, Mummy.

Helene Because I'd hate you to be unhappy. I'd give up every second of my joy having you home if it meant that –

Osvald   Tell me, mother. Are you really happy that
I'm here?

Helene   Am I happy? How can you ask me that?

Osvald   Isn't it the same for you if I'm here or not?

Helene   You have the heart to say that to your mother,
Osvald?

Osvald   You seem to have managed very well here without
me. Most of my life, in fact.

Helene   Yes . . . I've lived without you. That's true.

Short pause.

Osvald   Mummy. Can I come and sit with you?

Helene   Of course. Sit down here, my baby boy.

Osvald   There's something I have to tell you.

Helene   Of course.

Osvald   Because . . . I can't keep it secret any longer.

Helene   What? What is it?

Osvald   I couldn't write it in a letter, and since I've been
here I've . . .

Helene   Osvald, you can tell me.

Osvald   Yesterday and today I just tried to push it out of
my mind – but I couldn't.

Helene   Tell me what's happening, Osvald, please.

Osvald   Sit down. And I'll try . . . You know how I've been
so tired, from the train and the boat . . .

Helene   Yes. What about it?

Osvald   What's wrong with me it's not – not a normal kind
of tiredness.

Helene   There's nothing wrong with you, my baby.

Osvald Sit down! Mummy . . . I'm not ill, not in a normal sense of the word, I'm . . . Sick. I'm . . . broken. Inside. I'll never paint again.

Helene Osvald, no. Look at me. Look at me, baby, that's not true.

Osvald I'll never work again. Never, never – like the living dead.

Helene My unhappy boy. What's happened to you?

Osvald I don't know, I don't know . . . Mummy, look at me, believe me: I never lived a wild life out there.

Helene I know, baby, I know.

Osvald Then why is this happening to me?

Helene Nothing is happening to you, Osvald. You're just very tired. In a few days, in a week, you'll feel much better.

Osvald No, I won't.

Helene Why? Tell me, Osvald. Tell me what's happening.

Osvald It started just after I was home last time. It started when I got back to Paris. I began to get the most incredible headaches. In the back of my skull. It was like an iron ring being tightened around my neck – the pressure, the pain, in my skull. At first I thought it was those migraines I got, as a child.

Helene Yes.

Osvald But then it stopped me working. I wanted to paint – I was inspired – but then it took over. I felt dizzy. I couldn't focus on anything – the canvas – even the room was spinning. I could barely stand. It stole all my power, all my – passion . . . I called the doctor to the apartment. And he told me the truth.

Helene What?

Osvald   He was a specialist. He knew. At first, he asked me
so many questions – things that seemed strange, irrelevant –

Helene   But he found out what was wrong?

Osvald   Yes he did. He said I had . . . I've got . . .

Helene   What? . . . What?

Osvald   That I'm . . . infected.

Helene   . . .What does that mean?

Osvald   He said infected from birth, mother. He said it's
the sins of the father . . . The sins of the father visited on the
children.

Helene   Oh.

Osvald   Syphilis, Mummy.

Short pause.

I nearly knocked that bastard out. But I didn't – I just told
him: 'That can't be true. That's not true.' He said the
symptoms were clear, the way it presented. And so I got all
your letters, I read him page after page about Daddy.

Helene   And then?

Osvald   Then he backed down. Said he'd got it wrong. Not
about the disease but the cause of . . . transmission. That the
way I'd been living . . . with my friends . . . My free life, my
happy – . . . It's my fault. I've brought it all on myself . . .

Helene   Please don't think that, Osvald, please . . .

Osvald   I must have got it like that. There's no other way
he said. I was so reckless . . . I wish I had inherited it – that it
wasn't my fault, that I hadn't done this, but it was me. And
it's incurable. And I can't go back and change it. I've
wrecked it all: my health, my work, my life.

Helene   No, no, my darling boy, it's not what you think.

Osvald   And to cause you such pain, Mother. So many times I wished you didn't love me at all.

Helene   You're my boy. You're all I possess in the whole world. There's no one else but you.

Osvald   Yes I feel it. When I'm here with you, I feel it. But now we have to stop talking, Mummy. I can't think about it for long. Can I have a drink?

Helene   A drink? Of course. What would you like?

Osvald   Anything.

Helene   Careful, Osvald.

Osvald   Don't deny me, Mother. I need to drown these thoughts. It's so dark in here.

Helene (*calling out*)   Regine.

Osvald   This endless rain. Week after week after week. Never the sun.

Helene   You won't go away from me again? Regine!

Osvald   I don't know. I can't think. It's better I don't think at all.

Regine *is here.*

Scene Ten

Regine   You called, madam?

Helene   It's too dark in here.

Regine   Yes, madam.

Helene   Don't turn away from me, Osvald, please. Regine, get us a bottle of champagne.

Regine   Yes, madam.

Osvald   That's it, Mummy. I knew you wouldn't let me go thirsty.

Helene   How can I can deny you anything now?

Osvald   Is that true? Do you mean that?

Helene   What?

Osvald   You won't deny me anything?

Helene   But, Osvald . . .

Osvald   Shh. Shh, Mummy.

Regine (*indicating the champagne*)   Shall I open it?

Osvald   Yes.

Helene   What do you mean, Osvald darling, when you say I can't deny you anything?

Osvald   Let's have a drink. Together.

Helene   I won't – thank you.

Osvald   Yes you will.

What do you think of Regine, Mummy?

Helene   What do you mean?

Osvald   She's incredible, isn't she?

Helene   Osvald . . . You don't know her as well as I do.

Osvald   So?

Helene   Regine lived at home for too long, before I brought her here.

Osvald   But she's so beautiful, Mother. Look at her.

Helene   She is. She is but . . . she also . . . has her flaws.

Osvald   Well, don't we all.

Helene   She . . . I'm very fond of her. I – love her. And I'm responsible for her. I don't want anyone to hurt her.

Osvald   Mother, listen. I know now: Regine is the only who can save me.

Helene   Why do you say that?

Osvald   I can't bear all this pain. Not on my own.

Helene   You can share it with your mother.

Osvald   That's what I thought. That's why I came. But it won't work. I have to get away from you. I don't want you to see this.

Helene   A sick child needs their mother.

Osvald   It's not just the sickness, Mother. If it were only that I'd stay with you. Because you're my best friend. You're my best friend in the whole world.

Helene   I am! I am, aren't I?

Osvald   But it's everything thing else: the shame, the guilt – and the fear – this fear that grips me.

Helene   Fear? Fear of what?

Osvald   I can't describe it. I don't want to talk about it.

Helene   Champagne! That will make my poor boy happy. Chase those rainy clouds away. (*To* **Regine**, *who is pouring another glass.*) No, the whole bottle. (*To* **Osvald**.) You think we don't know how to live in the country? Come on!

Regine *passes the bottle to* **Osvald**, *who presents her to his mother.*

Osvald   Isn't she incredible? Huh? God: look at her. Look at you! So . . . Healthy. *Strong*.

Helene   Calm down, sweetness. Let's just – talk about this.

Osvald   You don't know this, Mother, but . . . How do I say this? I did something to Regine that I shouldn't have.

Helene   You –?

Osvald   I'm being silly – over-the-top. It's all very innocent. And anyway, now's the time I make it right.

Helene   What did you do?

Osvald   The last time I was home, Regine was asking me all the time about Paris – weren't you? And I was telling her all about it, and I just found myself saying: 'Do you want to come?' To Paris. And she just went bright red.

Regine   Sir . . .

Osvald   Didn't you? And she said: 'I'd love that.' And I just said, 'Yes, let's do that' – or something like that.

Helene   And?

Osvald   Of course I just forgot all about it. But when I got back – day before yesterday – I asked her if she was happy I'm home 'til Christmas, and you looked sort of hurt – or sad. And then she said to me: 'But what about my trip to Paris?' You see, she'd taken everything I'd said completely seriously. Hadn't you? She's been thinking about me the whole time I've been away. She's even learning French – aren't you?

Helene   I see.

Osvald   And that's when I saw it, Mother. This luscious, glowing woman – full of life. (*To* **Regine**.) I'd never really seen you before – then there you were, arms wide open, ready to receive me.

Helene   Osvald . . .

Osvald   And I knew it: that she could save me. I see it in her. The lifeforce.

Helene   Lifeforce?

Osvald   The joy of being alive. (*To* **Regine**.) Get another glass.

Regine   Madam's glass is here.

Osvald   One for yourself.

A moment: **Regine** *looks at* **Helene**.

Osvald   Well?

Regine   Does madam wish . . .?

Helene   Get the glass.

Regine *fetches a third glass.*

Osvald   Look at her move! Such strength – confidence.

Helene   This isn't going to happen, Osvald.

Osvald   It already has. There's nothing you can say. (*Indicating* **Regine** *should sit with them.*) Come here.

Helene   What do you mean? The 'joy of being alive'?

Osvald   *Joie de vivre*, Mother. They don't go in for it much round here.

Helene   But don't you feel that joy with me?

Osvald   I don't feel it here. This country, this house. You.

Helene   Don't say that.

Osvald   It's everyone here. Life only makes sense if it's suffering. It's a curse. A punishment for us sinners – all we deserve.

Helene   I know that's how we live.

Osvald   But out there, there's something else. Bliss, *joy*. Everything I paint comes from that joy. From light, from Sunday afternoons, from laughter, from love. That's why I'm so scared of staying here with you.

Helene   Please don't be scared of me.

Osvald   If I stay here I'm afraid the light inside me will go out.

Helene   Do you really believe that?

Osvald   There's too much darkness here, Mother.

Helene   But now I can see.

Osvald   See what?

Helene   For the first time I can see it. And now I will speak.

Regine   Perhaps I should leave?

Helene   No, stay. (*Gathering* **Osvald** *and* **Regine** *together.*) Now I will speak. I'll tell you everything. Everything. And then you can choose. (*Kissing him.*) Osvald. (*Kissing her.*) Regine . . .

Father Manders *is here.*

Osvald (*alerting her*)   Mother.

Scene Eleven

Manders   Well, we've had a very special time down there.

Osvald   We've had a special time up here.

Manders   We must help Engstrand with his sailors' home. Regine must move to town and help him.

Regine   I don't want to. Thank you.

Manders (*noticing her*)   You're here? You're drinking?

Regine   *Pardonnez moi.*

Osvald   Regine is coming back with me, Father.

Manders   What? With you?

Osvald   Yes, to Paris. As my wife. If she wants to.

Manders   The Lord God please have mercy.

Regine   It wasn't my idea, Father.

Osvald   Just as long as we're together. If we stay here –

Regine   Stay here?

Manders   What have you done, Helene?

Helene   You're not going to Paris, you're not staying here, because now I can speak and now you must know.

Manders   Wait! You're not going to . . . You can't.

Helene   I can and I will. It's not the truth that kills us.

Osvald   Just say it, Mother! What are you hiding?

Regine   Madam, listen! There's people outside. Can you hear them?

Osvald   What's happening? Where's that light coming from? On the water – in the sky.

Regine   The children's home's on fire.

Helene   On fire?!

Manders   Impossible. That's impossible. I've just come from there.

Osvald (*exiting*)   Father's memory! Bring my coat!

Helene (*to* **Regine**)   Get his coat. Get a hat. They'll be nothing left. Look.

Manders   It's punishment from God. He's punishing this house of sin.

Helene   Yes.

Manders   And you let me not insure it.

III

Helene   Soon they'll be nothing left.

Regine   The roof's falling in.

Helene   Why did Osvald go? There's nothing he can do.

Regine   I'll go after him.

Helene   No. Let me.

She goes to look for **Osvald**.

Manders   This is the worst night of my life.

Regine   I'm so sorry, Father.

Manders   I can't talk about it. I can't think about it.

Regine   How did it start?

Manders   Don't ask me. Your father . . .

Regine   What about him? Was he there?

Manders   He was, he . . . – I pray he got out in time.

Scene Twelve

Engstrand *appears.*

Engstrand   Hello, Father.

Manders   Engstrand. Thank God.

Engstrand   I'm so sorry this is happening.

Manders   Thank you.

Engstrand   I'm so sorry this is happening to you.

Manders   Thank you. To me?

Engstrand (*to* **Regine**)   To think it was me that asked the Father down there, my child. To lead a night of humble prayer. How would I know what he'd do?

Manders   I'd do?

Engstrand   The Father was the only one who touched the candles, see.

Manders   Wait – no, I wasn't.

Engstrand   I saw it with my own eyes. How he snuffed one out with the fingers, and chucked it on a pile of wood shavings.

Manders   Did I?

Engstrand   Yes.

Manders   You saw that?

Engstrand   Yes.

Manders   But I never put out candles with my fingers.

Engstrand   I was surprised myself. Doesn't that hurt? (*To* **Regine**.) And of course he hadn't insured it.

Manders   Exactly. How do you know that?

Engstrand   Not insured and then he sets it all on fire. It's tragic.

Manders   Stop. Stop, Engstrand.

Engstrand   The newspapers won't be kind. Nor the council. A charitable institution – for orphans – burnt to the ground. (*To* **Regine**.) They might turn on him again.

Manders   My God.

Engstrand   Another scandal.

Manders   Oh my God.

Helene (*returning*)   I can't see him.

Manders   When they find out . . .

Helene   I'm worried he's trying to fight it.

Manders (*to* **Helene**)   I need to talk to you.

Helene   Well, you won't have to make that speech tomorrow now. It's for the best. That children's home wouldn't have done anyone any good.

Regine   What about the children?

Helene   It served its function. Now it's gone. (*To* **Manders**.) Are you getting the boat tonight?

Manders   In an hour, but –

Helene   Then take everything with you. Deeds, account books, contracts. I don't want to see them again.

Manders   We need to discuss this.

Helene I'll write to you. Make you executor.

Manders But the legacy will change completely.

Helene *makes a dismissive gesture.*

Manders Well, I could arrange it so the land goes to the parish. That's still worth a lot. And there's the money in the bank – and the interest. It must be put to good use – for the benefit of the town. I could launch a new project.

Helene I don't care.

Engstrand The good of the town? What about my sailors' home, Father?

Manders We have to think carefully.

Engstrand Don't think, Father. Act. Those poor boys at sea.

Manders You don't understand. The fire. They'll be an inquest – attacks, accusations. I could lose my seat on the council. I could lose my parish.

Engstrand Not if I have anything to do with it.

Manders What do you mean?

Engstrand Jakob Engstrand would never abandon a generous patron in a time of need. Jakob Engstrand is a guardian angel, watching over you. He takes the burdens from the shoulders of others. I've done it before. Let me eat the sin, Father.

Manders How?

Engstrand Perhaps I didn't see you snuff that candle, Father. Perhaps, it was me who snuffed the candle.

Manders But, Engstrand . . . you can't . . .

Engstrand Father, I insist.

Manders Redemption . . . Engstrand – Jakob – your sailors' home will have everything it needs. I'll see to that.

Your goodness is a rare and precious thing . . . Let's go.
Back to town – together.

Engstsrand   Thank you, Father. (*To* **Regine**.) Come on girl.
Come on. Come home. Daddy'll look after you.

Regine   *Non, merci.*

Engstrand   Well, if you change your mind, you know where
I am. In the house for wandering sailors I'll call 'Captain
Alving's Home'. I'll make sure that place, and all that goes
on inside, will be a fitting tribute to that man's life. *Au revoir.*

Manders   Come, dear Engstrand. And goodbye.

Manders *and* **Engstrand** *leave.* **Osvald** *has already returned.*

Scene Thirteen

Osvald *moves with restless, nervous energy.*

Osvald   What is 'Captain Alving's Home'?

Helene   A home for sailors he and the Father are building

Osvald   It'll burn down.

Helene   What do you mean?

Osvald   Just like that one did. They all burn down. Soon
they'll be nothing left of Father. I'm on fire too.

Helene   You shouldn't have gone down there.

Osvald   I wanted to save it.

Helene   You're sweating. (*Touching him to check his
temperature.*) You're burning up. Let's get you to bed.

Osvald   No. I never sleep – I just lie there pretending. But
I'll sleep soon enough.

Helene   You have to rest.

Osvald *pulls off his shirt.*

Osvald   It's coming. The fear. Lock all the doors.

Regine   Is Mr Alving ill?

Helene (*embracing him*)   I'm here, my baby. Shh, shh.
I'm here.

Osvald   Don't leave me. Please. And Regine too. (*To*
Regine.) Promise you won't leave me. Promise you'll help
me, that you'll . . . Help me out . . .

Regine   I don't understand what you –

Osvald   To stop it hurting. When I need it.

Helene   Osvald, your mother's here. Mummy's here
to help.

Osvald   My mother?! No. A mother can't help her son. Not
like that. (*To* **Regine**.) It has to be you. Come here, Regine.
(*Reaching out to her.*) Come here. Why do you always call me
sir? Why don't you use my name?

Regine   I don't think Mrs Alving would like it.

Helene   It's alright. Come and sit with us. Come.

Osvald   Come here.

Regine *sits with* **Helene** *and* **Osvald**. *Mother and son
embrace her.*

Helene   Yes. You can call him Osvald very soon. Because
now . . . (*To* **Osvald**.) I'm going to take your pain away. I'm
going to set you free.

Osvald   You?

Helene   Set you free from your shame.

Osvald   You can't.

Helene   When you talked about the joy of life – of *living* – I
suddenly saw everything in my life so clearly.

She stands. **Osvald** *and* **Regine** *remain entwined.*

Osvald   What did you see?

Helene   I wish you'd known your father when he was young – your age. He was so full of energy – of light. But then this beautiful child – because he was a child – got stuck, here, in this town, with these people, and their judgements and their shame. You said yourself what would happen if you stayed here.

Osvald   What do you mean?

Helene   And it was my fault too. I tried to be a good wife – I did – but I was so unhappy. I made it unbearable here. He had so much joy in him and there was nowhere for it to go. And so it . . . It went where it shouldn't. Into alcohol. Into other women. Into doing – what he did. Osvald, your father was a sick man. He was . . . broken. Long before you were born.

Osvald   But what you wrote to me. Your letters . . .?

Helene   I thought that loving him would bring you joy. Instead it brought you pain. But now you know the truth about him. And that it's not your fault. (*To* **Regine**.) You too, Regine. It's not your fault. Not you, his son. And not you, his daughter.

Pause.

There. So now you know.

Short pause.

It's alright.

Regine *pulls away from* **Osvald**.

Helene   It's alright.

Regine   So . . . my mother . . . That's what happened to my mother . . .

Helene   Your mother was . . . a good woman, Regine – she tried.

Regine   Mrs Alving, I'd like to be excused. With your permission, I want to leave now, please.

Helene   If you're sure that's what you want?

Regine   It's what I want.

Helene   Then you should go.

Osvald   Go? No, you belong here. With us. This is your home. We are your family. Yes? . . . Yes? . . . Yes?

Regine   Yes. (*Embracing him.*) Yes. *Merci, Monsieur Alving* . . . I can call you Osvald now.

She starts to pull away from **Osvald**.

Regine   But not the way I wanted. This is not what I wanted.

Osvald *won't let go of* **Regine**.

Helene (*to* **Regine**)   I know I haven't been straight with you.

Regine (*struggling with* **Osvald**)   No. No. (*To* **Helene**.) He's ill. He's sick. (*To* **Osvald**.) And we can't. *We can't.*

She pulls away from **Osvald**. *He continues to reach for her.*

I can't stay. I can't stay here.

Osvald   Not even for your brother?

Regine   I can't stay here with the sick.

Osvald   But I'm your blood.

Regine   I have to live. Everything's disgusting here. Everything is death. (*To* **Helene**.) Madam – Hel – . . . Madam. I can't stay here. I can't. I'm still young. People – men – they – like me.

Helene   Of course. Of course.

Regine   And I still have that joy.

Helene   Don't waste yourself, Regine.

Regine   I have to live.

Helene   We'll find you a man. A man will take you.

Regine   Does the Father know? Does the Father know about me?

Helene   He . . . does. He does.

Regine   Right. Right . . . The boat's not left. Father Manders will look after me. And that money he's giving out – I've as much right to it as that filthy old carpenter.

Helene   You have. You deserve it. And Engstrand owes you money too. It's your inheritance, Regine. Your birthright.

Regine *slowly pulls away from* **Helene**.

Regine   But you . . . You could have brought me up as family. Here. I could have been a Captain's daughter. I could have been so much – but you . . .

She picks up a bottle of champagne.

It doesn't matter. Now I'll drink my champagne. Cheers.

She drinks.

Here's to sir and madam.

She drinks.

(*To* **Helene**.) Cheers. Cheers!

Helene   Cheers. I need a glass . . .

Regine   No just drink it. Drink it. I'm not your maid.

Helene   Oh. I . . .

Regine   I said drink it.

Regine *pours champagne on* **Helene**.

Drink it. Drink it. There.

Pause.

Father Manders will look after me. And if that goes wrong, there's somewhere else that I can go.

Helene   Where?

Regine   'Captain Alving's Sailors' Home'.

Helene   No. No, you can't Regine.

Regine   Yes I can. Why not?

Helene   Because –. Listen to me: you'll get sick there, you'll die.

Regine   Maybe . . . But maybe not. *Adieu* 'Helene'.

She is leaving.

(*To* **Osvald**.) *Au revoir.*

She's gone.

Scene Fourteen

Osvald   Has she gone?

Helene   Come here, my baby boy. You must be in shock.

Osvald   Why?

Helene   About Regine. About your father. I'm scared it's all too much for you.

Osvald   No. It's a surprise. Nothing more.

Helene   But – it changes who you thought he was.

Osvald   What difference does that make to me?

Helene   Because – it changes who you think you are.

Osvald   Does it? I feel sorry for him. That he was so unhappy here. – Like I'd feel sorry for anyone.

Helene   He's not anyone, he's your father.

Osvald   Oh yes father. Father. Dad. All I have is one memory of him. He made me smoke, he made me sick.

Helene   But you loved him. He's your family – he's your blood.

Osvald   I didn't know him, so I didn't love him. That's the truth. It's nothing to do with blood.

Helene   Do you love me?

Osvald   I know you, that's different.

Helene   You know me. That's all?

Osvald   I know how much you think of me. And I'm grateful for that.

Helene *is winded by his words.*

Osvald   And I'm grateful for what you're going to do now. Now that I'm sick.

Helene   I could kiss your sickness, Osvald. It brought you home to me. And if you don't love me now, I'll earn it. I'll do anything, anything for you.

Osvald   You have to take away my fear. Promise me you'll do that.

Helene   Yes.

Osvald   Regine: she would have done it.

Helene   I'll do it. I'll take away your fear.

Osvald   Do you promise?

Helene   The dawn's coming. It's starting to get light. See? Soon you'll see the sun, Osvald. And feel it on your skin.

Osvald   I want the sun.

Helene   Yes.

Osvald   I want to live.

Helene   You will!

Osvald   I want that so much, Mummy.

Helene   You will. And you'll paint again. I know you will. You're free now – from your guilt, your shame.

Osvald Yes, yes. You took it all away.

Helene I did, didn't I?

Osvald There's one thing left for you to do.

Helene Tell me.

Osvald I'll tell you, as the sun comes up. And then you'll know – and I won't be scared anymore.

Helene What will I know?

Osvald You said you'd do anything.

Helene Yes.

Osvald You promised.

Helene You're all I live for.

Osvald Because you'll have to be strong. Strong for me.

Helene Just tell me!

Osvald Stop. Listen. No crying, no hysterics. Understand?

Helene I understand.

Osvald My disease . . . the headaches, the fatigue, that's not the end of it. No. It ends here. (*He points at his forehead.*) It takes root, and lies in wait, until it strikes.

Helene You mustn't say that, Osvald. The stress will –

Osvald Listen to me! . . . There's no way out of this. They're coming: the seizures. As the lesions spread on the brain . . . They soften it. They open it. Can you see it? Like cutting through soft velvet. Cherry red velvet . . . Parting.

Helene You don't know that it's spread there.

Osvald I had my first attack in Paris. Blacked out, completely. For hours. And when it passed that's when the fear began. The not knowing – when it'll strike again – how long I've got. I wish that I just had cancer. I could handle that. I'm not afraid to die.

Helene   Don't say that.

Osvald   And it's so degrading. Incapacitation. Can't feed myself, can't – clean myself. Like a baby.

Helene   My baby. With his mother to care for him.

Osvald   No. Never. That's exactly what I don't want. Understand? Trapped inside my body – for years – my hair still growing turning white – body wrinkling – withering away.

Helene   I'll be here for you.

Osvald   Not if you die first.

Helene   Osvald!

Osvald   You took Regine away from me. She would have helped me.

Helene   I can help you.

Osvald *holds up a small metal box.*

Helene   What's that?

Osvald   The doctor gave it to me. I made him.

Helene   What is it?

Osvald   Morphine powder.

Helene   Osvald, my sweet boy.

Osvald   Twelve capsules. But four should be enough.

Helene   Give that to me.

Osvald   Not yet.

Helene   You're killing me too.

Osvald   No: you must be strong. Regine would have done it. She wouldn't let me lie there.

Helene   She ran away.

Osvald   Disgusting – in my own filth – gurgling, dribbling.

Helene   Thank God she's not here.

Osvald   Now you must do it, Mummy.

Helene   Me?

Osvald   You're all I have left.

Helene   I gave you life. I gave birth to you.

Osvald   I didn't ask you to. I don't want my life. Take it back. Take it back.

Helene (*running from* **Osvald** *and calling out*)   Help. Help me. Somebody.

Osvald   Stop trying to leave me.

Helene   I have to get a doctor.

Osvald   No one's getting out and no one's getting in.

Helene   My baby, please.

Osvald   Is this what you call a mother's love? Leaving me in terror every day? Mummy. Mummy please.

Pause.

Helene   Here. Here's my hand.

Osvald   You'll do it?

Helene   If I have to.

Osvald   Thank you.

Helene   It won't come to that.

Osvald   Yes. Thank you, thank you. Let's be together. Live as long as we can. You and me.

Helene   Yes. Yes. Do you feel better now? More calm?

Osvald *nods. He's in her arms.*

Helene   I know it's been so hard for you. And I think you've made this up. You've imagined all of this, to try to cope with everything. To make sense of the pain. But you're home now. With Mummy. And you can rest. I'll do everything for you here. Just say the word – just point at something – like when you were little. Just point and it's yours. Mummy's here. Mummy's got you. No more fear. And no more pain. The sun's coming up. Can you see it? Can you see the sun?

Osvald (*quietly*)   I want the sun.

Helene   What, my baby?

Osvald   Give me the sun.

Helene   Osvald . . .?

Osvald (*weakly, almost lifeless*)   The sun . . . The sun . . .

Helene (*panicked*)   Osvald. Osvald!

Osvald   The sun.

Helene   Osvald, look at me. Come back to me. Talk to me.

Osvald   The sun.

Helene   Osvald. No.

Looking for the box of morphine capsules.

Where are they? Where are they?

She finds the metal box.

Osvald (*virtually inaudible*)   The sun . . . The sun . . .

Helene *holds the box in front of her.*

Helene   No. Never! . . . Yes . . . No . . . Yes . . .

The end.

For a complete listing of
Methuen Drama titles, visit:

www.bloomsbury.com/drama

Follow us on Twitter and keep up to date
with our news and publications

@MethuenDrama